OKLAHOMA

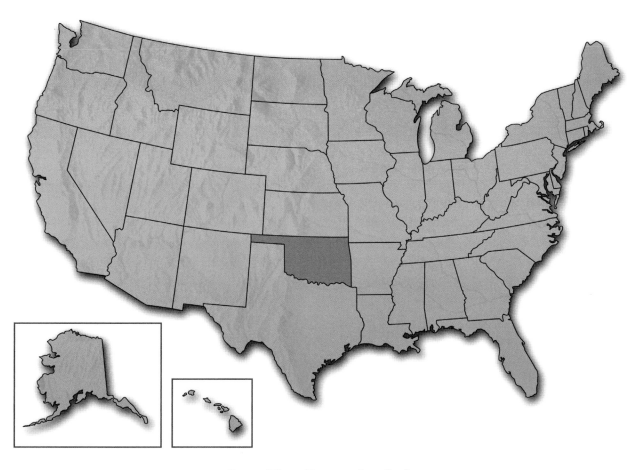

Leslie Strudwick

Published by Weigl Publishers Inc.
123 South Broad Street, Box 227
Mankato, MN   56002
USA
Web site: http://www.weigl.com

Library of Congress Cataloging-in-Publication Data

Strudwick, Leslie, 1970-
   Oklahoma / Leslie Strudwick.
     p. cm. -- (American states)
   Includes index.
   ISBN 1-930954-08-5 (lib.bdg. : alk. paper)
   1. Oklahoma--Juvenile literature. [1. Oklahoma] I. Title. II. Kid's guide to American states.

F694.3 S77 2001
976.6--dc21

2001022512

ISBN 1-930954-98-0 (pbk.)

Printed in the United States of America
1 2 3 4 5 6 7 8 9 10   05 04 03 02 01

Project Coordinator
Jennifer Nault
Substantive Editor
Rennay Craats
Copy Editor
Heather Kissock
Designers
Warren Clark
Terry Paulhus
Photo Researcher
Angela Lowen

Photograph Credits
Every reasonable effort has been made to trace ownership and to obtain permission to reprint copyright material. The publishers would be pleased to have any errors or omissions brought to their attention so that they may be corrected in subsequent printings.

Cover: Cowboy in Red Shirt (PhotoDisc Corporation), Storm Clouds (Digital Stock), **Jim Argo:** 6BL, 7B, 9B, 13T, 13BL, 13BR, 14B, 15BL, 20BL, 21B, 22T, 22BL; **Arkansas History Commission:** 18B; **Corbis Corporation:** 8BR, 26BL; **Corel Corporation:** 10T, 11M, 11B; **Curtis/The Image Finders:** 28T; **Steve Mulligan Photography:** 10BR, 10BL; **Oklahoma Department of Commerce:** 14T, 15T, 15BR; **Oklahoma Tourism/Fred W. Marvel:** 4T, 4BL, 5T, 5BL, 6T, 6BR, 7ML, 7MR, 8T, 8BL, 9T, 11T, 12T, 12BL, 12BR, 16T, 16B, 17T, 17BL, 17BR, 18T, 20T, 20BR, 21T, 22BR, 23B, 24T, 24M, 24B, 28B, 29T, 29B; **Photofest:** 4BR, 25T, 25BL, 25BR, 26T, 26BR; **Tulsa Metro Chamber of Commerce:** 23T; **University of Oklahoma:** 27T, 27B; **Western History Collections, University of Oklahoma Library:** 19T, 19BL, 19BR.

CONTENTS

Robbers Cave State Park in Oklahoma is where outlaws such as Jesse James once stored their loot.

INTRODUCTION

"Brand new state! Brand new state, gonna treat you great!" This first line from Oklahoma's state song displays the enthusiasm Oklahomans have for their home state. The song is from the popular Rodgers and Hammerstein musical, *Oklahoma!*, which is based on the creation and settlement of the state.

Although Oklahoma is usually thought to consist of flat prairies, the state is truly breathtaking. Its terrain is **diverse**, with mountainous land as well as vast areas of level plains. Over history, Oklahoma's land has been inhabited by Native Peoples, African Americans, pioneers, cowboys, and outlaws. All have contributed to the state's rich past, paving the way to the present.

QUICK FACTS

Before the state song was Rodgers and Hammerstein's "Oklahoma!," it was "Oklahoma (A Toast)" by Harriet Parker Camden.

The barite rose, a rock shaped like a rose, is the state rock.

The state colors are green and white.

Oklahoma!, the musical, won the Pulitzer Prize for drama in 1944.

Oklahoma City is the transportation center of the state.

QUICK FACTS

The state motto, which is in Latin, is *Labor Omnia Vincit*. It translates as "Labor Conquers all Things."

From 1890 to 1910, Guthrie was the capital of Oklahoma. In 1910, Oklahoma City was named the capital city.

The corners of Oklahoma, New Mexico, and Colorado all meet at one point.

Getting There

The state of Oklahoma lies in the south-central portion of the United States. Surrounding Oklahoma are six other states. Arkansas and Missouri lie to the east, Kansas and Colorado are north, New Mexico is west, and Texas shares Oklahoma's entire southern border.

Visitors traveling by automobile can access the state via one of three separate interstate highways. Residents in the state are served by about 112,524 miles of highway. The Amtrak rail system also services Oklahoma with 3,348 miles of track. For those who prefer to fly, there are two international airports in the state—one in Oklahoma City and the other in Tulsa. Oklahoma also has about 320 airports, most of which are privately owned.

Oklahoma Location Map

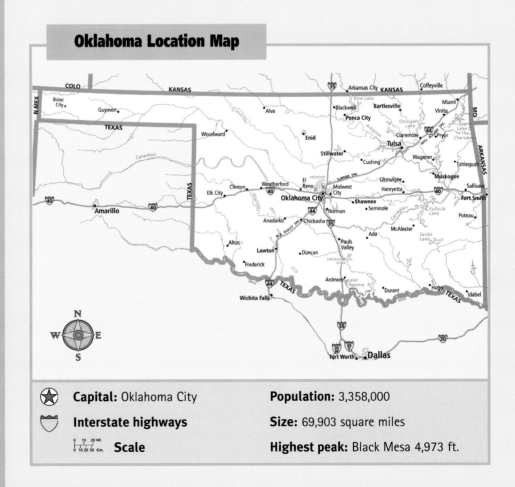

⭐ **Capital:** Oklahoma City

🛡 **Interstate highways**

Scale
0 10 20 Mi.
0 10 20 30 Km.

Population: 3,358,000

Size: 69,903 square miles

Highest peak: Black Mesa 4,973 ft.

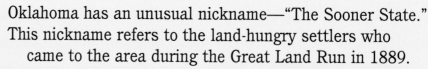

Oklahoma has an unusual nickname—"The Sooner State." This nickname refers to the land-hungry settlers who came to the area during the Great Land Run in 1889. Although much of Oklahoma's land was reserved for Native Americans, the government made a plot of land available to new settlers. Newcomers were told to line up at the Oklahoma border and, at the signal, race to claim the land. Those who jumped the starting gun were called Sooners.

"Boomer's Paradise" is yet another early nickname for the state of Oklahoma. This name refers to the people who illegally entered Native-American territory. They set up homes and communities on these reserved lands. These nicknames serve as reminders of Oklahoma's early history, when Native Peoples and settlers were wrestling over land and resources.

The state flag has a blue background with a Native-American shield bearing a pipe and an olive branch.

QUICK FACTS

At 69,903 square miles, Oklahoma is the twentieth largest state in the nation.

After the land runs, many settlers found the climate and soil suitable for growing wheat. Today, wheat is grown and harvested throughout the state of Oklahoma.

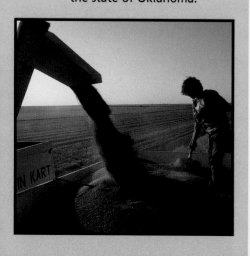

Oklahoma was originally settled by people who arrived on horseback. Today, residents and visitors can access most of the state by vehicle. The I-35, a key road in Oklahoma, runs from north to south across the state.

QUICK FACTS

In 1909, Oklahoma formed the first Boy Scout troop in the United States.

The movie *Twister*, a thrilling film about tornado chasers, was filmed in Oklahoma—a state known for its tornadoes.

There is an oil well under the Capitol in Oklahoma City.

Many Oklahomans have become famous astronauts. They include Gordon Cooper Jr., Owen Garriott, William Pogue, Thomas Stafford, and Shannon Lucid.

Thomas Stafford

Oklahoma was one of the last states to join the Union. It was admitted on November 16, 1907, becoming the forty-sixth state. The state retains much of its early Native-American **heritage**, with many place-names and people of Native-American origins.

From the Native Peoples, who set up the first system of government, to the Europeans, who left their countries in search of new farming opportunities, Oklahoma has been home to many. Today, the state is an interesting blend of traditional and modern influences. Modern-day cowboys, rodeos, and country music singers offer a link to the state's past. Its bright future is foretold in its large, modern, and highly-developed cities.

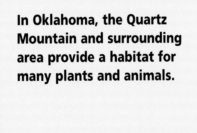

In Oklahoma, the Quartz Mountain and surrounding area provide a habitat for many plants and animals.

The Ozark Mountains have many natural wonders, including amazing rock formations and waterfalls.

LAND AND CLIMATE

The land in the Sooner State is great and varied. It offers **fertile** farmland and forested mountain ranges. Elevations in the state range from 300 to 5,000 feet above sea level. The Ouachita Mountains, in Oklahoma's southeast, boast steep ridges and valleys. The Red River Plains, on the other hand, are low and flat. The High Plains are just that—high. The land in this northwestern region is higher than the mountains to the east. Other parts of Oklahoma, such as the Ozark Plateau in the northeast, are made up of broad, flat-topped hills and narrow river valleys.

Oklahoma's climate is as varied as its landscape. During the winter, southern regions enjoy spring-like temperatures, while areas of the **Panhandle** are covered in as much as 12 inches of snow. Beyond the Panhandle, Oklahoma summers are long and hot, with mild and short winters. The state experiences many droughts and tornadoes. In fact, dozens of tornadoes touch down in Oklahoma each year.

Tornadoes usually strike Oklahoma during the months of April and May.

Oklahoma has about 500 named rivers and creeks.

NATURAL RESOURCES

Oklahoma has an abundance of natural resources within its boundaries. Forests in the Ouachita Mountains and along the Sandstone Hills provide a home for wildlife. These forests also provide trees for the lumber industry. On the prairies, crops such as oats, corn, and soybeans are grown in the northeast. Fields of wheat, barley, hay, and cotton are grown and harvested in the center of the state. Many regions are ideal for raising cattle. Of the 34 million acres of farmland, about two-thirds are rangeland for livestock.

Water is another important resource in the state. About 100 natural and 200 artificial lakes dot the state. Most of the lakes are fed by flowing rivers and streams. The two largest rivers are the Red and the Arkansas.

In terms of money brought into the state, mining is the main industry in Oklahoma. Large deposits of salt, coal, and gypsum are mined. Other minerals found in the state include limestone, sand, gravel, granite, and clay. Oil and natural gas are also found in the earth. Oklahoma ranks third in the country in the production of natural gas.

There are about 2 million acres of pine forests used for lumber and paper production in Oklahoma.

PLANTS AND ANIMALS

Forests and grasslands dominate much of Oklahoma's landscape. The state's largest forested areas are located in the east. More than 130 varieties of trees thrive in the state. Among these are longleaf pine, cottonwood, oak, hickory, juniper, and willow.

The Plains regions, when not supporting new farm crops, are covered in different kinds of grasses and wild plants. Sagebrush is common in this area, along with gramma, buffalo, Indian, and mesquite grasses. Wild flowers can be found in this area, too. They include black-eyed Susans, poppy mallows, wild indigos, prairie coneflowers, violets, wild roses, and prickly pear cacti.

The Tallgrass Prairie Preserve covers 37,000 acres of land north of Pawkuska. It maintains some of the state's original prairies.

QUICK FACTS

The state flower is the mistletoe.

From 1988 to 1995, Oklahoma reduced the amount of toxic chemicals put into the environment by 55 percent.

The redbud is Oklahoma's state tree. It was adopted in 1937.

In addition to the millions of head of cattle that roam the land, Oklahoma is home to many animals. Copperhead and cottonmouth snakes can be found slithering in the area. Oklahoma also has a poisonous snake—the rattlesnake. Prairie dogs, raccoons, deer, antelope, and both gray and fox squirrels also live in the region.

Prairie dogs are known for their piercing, bark-like cry.

Many different birds nest in the state, including blue jays, mockingbirds, orioles, crows, roadrunners, and robins. Cardinals, meadowlarks, quails, wild turkeys, prairie chickens, and pheasants are also commonly found in the area.

If people head to any of the state's many lakes and rivers, they will be sharing the waterways with a large variety of fish. Bass, catfish, carp, sunfish, drumfish, and paddlefish can all be found in Oklahoma's waters.

Although roadrunners will eat plants, insects and reptiles make up most of their diet.

The National Cowboy and Western Heritage Center's chronicles the history of the West through its art.

QUICK FACTS

Tourists in Oklahoma
City can visit the International Photography Hall of Fame and Museum and the National Softball Hall of Fame.

In Tulsa, the Gilcrease Museum houses a large collection of Western art and artifacts.

Events such as rodeos and horse shows draw people to Oklahoma.

TOURISM

Vacationers come to the Sooner State to enjoy its natural beauty, outdoor activities, and much more. Oklahoma has more artificial lakes than any other state—more than 200. In the summer, tourists can visit any number of these lakes to enjoy fishing, boating, water-skiing, sailing, or windsurfing. Resorts can also be found along some of the larger lakes, where patrons can golf, play tennis, dine in great restaurants, and stay in cottages or hotels.

Nature lovers and history buffs will be pleasantly surprised by Oklahoma's many attractions and recreational areas. Visitors can choose to explore any of the state's two national parks, thirty-two state parks, twenty-eight state recreation areas, or forty-eight wildlife management areas. There are many museums and cultural sites in the state, too. At the Anadarko Basin Museum Of Natural History in Elk City, visitors can view rocks, minerals, and fossils. The National Cowboy and Western Heritage Museum in Oklahoma City is a large attraction that features just about everything related to cowboy culture. This museum boasts artwork and displays that preserve the state's Western heritage.

The Oklahoma Department of Wildlife Conservation keeps the tradition of fishing in Oklahoma alive by teaching fishing skills to children.

Since the General Motors plant in Oklahoma City opened in 1979, it has manufactured about 5 million vehicles.

INDUSTRY

Along with agriculture and mining, manufacturing is a key industry. Oklahoma manufactures machinery, transportation equipment, food products, and rubber and plastic products. The state also manufactures electrical equipment, mobile homes, and glass and clay products. Tulsa and Oklahoma counties are considered the most important manufacturing areas.

Oklahoma's **diversified** industry base keeps the economy quite stable, even in times of failed crops and low oil or cattle prices. Many oil-producing areas often have another strong industry to balance the economy. For example, while Tulsa may have more than 1,000 oil-based companies in the city, it also has a strong **aviation** and aerospace industry.

QUICK FACTS

Oklahoma is known as a livestock state. There are more than 5 million cattle raised in the state.

Petroleum, natural gas, and coal account for 95 percent of the state's mining **revenues**.

Oklahoma manufactures oil and gas-related machinery. This includes equipment used in oil extraction, such as pumps, pipes, and valves.

The petroleum industry has been an important part of Oklahoma's economy for more than seventy years.

Oklahoma's aerospace industry employs about 143,000 people.

GOODS AND SERVICES

Many of the finished products manufactured in Oklahoma are transported to other parts of the country. Three national interstate highways cross Oklahoma. The state also has miles of railroad tracks to transport goods into and out of the state.

Oklahoma's stable and strong economy provides its residents with an affordable lifestyle. Compared to other cities in the United States, many goods and services are cheaper in Oklahoma City. On average, it would cost a person 28 percent more to live in Los Angeles and 52 percent more to live in Boston than it does to live in Oklahoma City. Oklahoma City and Tulsa are the least expensive cities for housing among seventy-five major cities in the United States. Doing business in Oklahoma is also less expensive, which attracts new companies to the state.

QUICK FACTS

The state of Oklahoma spends the largest portion of its budget on services such as education, highways, public welfare, and hospitals.

Oklahoma's first railroad, the Katy, was built between 1870 and 1872.

There are about 84,000 farms in Oklahoma. Farmland takes up nearly 34 million acres of land, with 44 percent of that land used to raise crops. The rest is mostly used for grazing livestock.

Wheat covers 33 percent of the state's total cropland.

About 230,000 students attend public colleges and universities in Oklahoma.

The production of electrical equipment, especially for communications, is an important industry in Oklahoma.

Food products are important to Oklahoma's economy. Flour mills operate in Blackwell, Shawnee, and Enid. Canneries package or freeze fruits and vegetables in many of the state's eastern cities. Creameries, ice cream plants, and bakeries supply treats and sweets to Oklahomans statewide. Meats are other important goods in the state. Meat packaging plants are found in many Oklahoma cities, including Tulsa, Durant, Oklahoma City, and Ada.

Newspaper publishing, which is part of the communications industry, is an important activity in Oklahoma. Besides the 230 newspapers published in the state, Oklahomans can also keep up with news and current events by tuning in to any of the state's 140 radio stations. Residents also have 20 local television stations from which to choose.

QUICK FACTS

There are more than 620,000 students attending about 1,400 public schools in Oklahoma.

Between 2000 and 2001, the state budget **allotted** more than $1.3 billion for higher education.

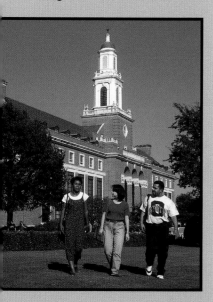

Biotechnology is an important industry in Oklahoma. One company in the state, Inoveon, has developed a way to detect the onset of blindness in people with diabetes.

FIRST NATIONS

Early Native Peoples, referred to as Mound Builders, lived close to the Arkansas-Oklahoma border from 800 to 1400 AD. Traces of the Mound Builders can still be found from central Georgia to southern Mississippi. The Mound Builders built large hills out of earth and used them as platforms for homes and as sites for their temples. Digging out the mounds has resulted in many finds. **Archeologists** have uncovered pottery, textiles, and metalwork that display a high level of skill.

When the Europeans arrived in the mid-1500s, there were a number of Native-American groups living across Oklahoma. Together, these groups were known as the Plains Indians. In the east, the Kiowa, the Plains Apache, and the Comanche, hunted bison on the prairie. The Caddo, Wichita, and Pawnee built villages in the region, and the Osage and Quapaw also lived in the Oklahoma area.

Archeologists have found many artifacts left by the early Spiro culture near the Spiro Mounds.

QUICK FACTS

The Spiro Mounds peoples had a highly developed culture. They had a large trading network, a religious center, and a political system.

When the Five Civilized Tribes were **relocated** to Oklahoma, they had to walk from their homelands in the southeastern United States. The route they were forced to take has become known as the Trail of Tears.

About 15,000 Native Peoples walked the Trail of Tears. Many died along the way.

When Native Americans were relocated, they were told that the new land in Oklahoma would be theirs "as long as grass shall grow and rivers run."

Spiro Mounds can still be found near Poteau. The largest mound is 33 feet high and 400 feet long.

The Cherokee Heritage Center accurately re-creates the early Cherokee lifestyle.

QUICK FACTS

A log cabin in Akins was occupied by Sequoyah, a Cherokee who developed a system of reading and writing in the Cherokee language in 1821.

The Cherokee Nation awarded Chief Sequoyah a medal and a lifetime pension for his contribution to the Cherokee culture.

After European settlement and the American Civil War, the Plains Indians were forced to move west, and five groups from the east were brought to the Oklahoma region. In order to make room for settlers, Native Peoples were pressured to move to land in present-day Oklahoma, known as Indian Territory. In 1842, several thousand Seminole were moved to Oklahoma. Along with the Seminole, the Cherokee, Chicksaw, Choctaw, and Creek set up their own system of government—it was the first organized system of government in Oklahoma. They were referred to as the "Five Civilized Tribes."

Later, more Native Peoples moved to the region, and about sixty groups soon shared the land. Still, Native Peoples had lost most of their land in Oklahoma by 1907. Today, thirty-five tribal governments are based in the state.

The Wichita's village structures were built by the women of the group.

Although Francisco Vásquez de Coronado explored Oklahoma, he never settled the area.

EXPLORERS AND MISSIONARIES

The first written history of Oklahoma dates back to 1541. Spanish explorers called *conquistadors* came to North America during the mid-1500s hoping to find gold and silver. Explorer Francisco Vásquez de Coronado was the first European to enter the Oklahoma area. Other Spanish explorers followed, all in search of the **fabled** golden Seven Cities of Cíbola. Although no golden city was ever found, Coronado claimed the western part of the Mississippi Valley for Spain. Another Spanish explorer, Hernando de Soto, laid claim to the lower Mississippi Valley for Spain. But Spain quickly lost control of the region to France.

In 1682, René-Robert Cavelier, also known as Sieur de La Salle, traveled south from the Great Lakes to the mouth of the Mississippi at the Gulf of Mexico. On behalf of the King of France, he claimed all the lands drained by the Mississippi River and its **tributaries**—this included present-day Oklahoma. French fur traders quickly made their way to the Oklahoma area, settling along the Red and Arkansas Rivers.

Hernando de Soto traveled through much of the United States on a quest for riches.

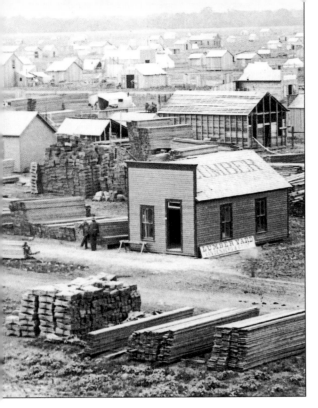

Less than a month after the first land run, the settlers of Oklahoma City set up a system of government and began building permanent homes.

QUICK FACTS

After the American Civil War, great cattle drives were run south from Texas up to the north and east of the United States. The cattle were driven right through Oklahoma. During this time, Oklahoma was part of the "Wild West."

After the first land run of 1889, there were more land runs. Each one took parts of Indian Territory from the Native Peoples.

The largest land run was in 1893, when 6 million acres were opened for settlement.

EARLY SETTLERS

Much of Oklahoma's early settlement was slow to develop because the government had reserved parts of its land for Indian Territory. But the Indian Territory grew quickly between 1870 and 1889, with ranching, railroad building, and mining being key activities. With increased pressure from settlers who wanted to move farther west, much of Indian Territory was opened up for European settlement in 1889.

A date was set for April 22, 1889, when 2 million acres would become available to homesteaders. At noon that day, a single shot marked the beginning of the land run. Fifty thousand people rushed to stake their land claims. In just one day, Oklahoma City was created. Incredibly, about 10,000 people pitched their tents and set up shelters in this area. Another 15,000 stopped at present-day Guthrie. This new town became the state's first capital.

Many of the early settlers' dwellings in Oklahoma were made out of sod. Sod houses were constructed from stacked layers of squarely-cut earth, shaped much like bricks. Settlers had to build sod houses because it was difficult to find trees on the plains.

Russians contributed to Oklahoma's early settlement. Some of their buildings, such as churches, can still be found in the state.

QUICK FACTS

Many African Americans came to Oklahoma to take part in the land runs. Shortly after the land runs, there were twenty-five African-American towns in the Indian Territory.

Of the sixty-seven Native-American groups that reside in the state, thirty-five have their headquarters in the state of Oklahoma.

POPULATION

Oklahoma's population is growing at a steady pace. More than 3.3 million people call the Sooner State home. Almost 70 percent of the population lives in urban areas—in cities or towns. There are twenty-five cities with populations of more than 15,000 people.

The residents of the Sooner State come from many different **ethnic** backgrounds. About 82 percent are of European ancestry, 7 percent are African American, and 1 percent are of either Asian or Pacific Island ancestry. Slightly more than 9 percent of the population are Hispanic American—with some belonging to another ethnic background. Compared to the national average of slightly less than 1 percent, the state has a relatively large Native-American community. With Native Americans making up about 8 percent of the state's total population, Oklahoma ranks third in the nation—following Alaska and New Mexico—for its percentage of Native Americans.

Oklahoma's Hispanic-American population more than doubled in the 1990s. By the end of the decade, it had increased from 4 percent to 9 percent of the state's total population.

The historic Washita County Courthouse is known as the "Grandfather of Oklahoma Courthouses."

QUICK FACTS

There are seventy-seven counties in the state, each run by three commissioners.

The cities and towns of the Sooner State are governed by a mayor or council manager along with a city council.

In 1907, a state constitution was approved upon Oklahoma entering the Union.

The Oklahoma Capitol was designed to resemble classical Greek and Roman architecture.

POLITICS AND GOVERNMENT

Oklahoma's government consists of three branches: the executive, the legislative, and the judicial. The governor heads the executive branch and appoints the secretary of state, the secretary of finance, and other state commissioners.

The Senate and House of Representatives make up the legislative branch. The 101 members of the House of Representatives along with the 48 Senate members make the laws of the state, but residents may also **propose** new laws.

The judicial branch is made up of the supreme court, the court of criminal appeals, and the court of appeals. It is the duty of each of the judges within these courts to interpret the laws of the state.

CULTURAL GROUPS

Native Peoples were the first group to live in the Oklahoma area. Today, they work to preserve their cultures and customs. Traditional dance exhibitions and large gatherings called **powwows** are held every summer and fall across the state.

The cowboy culture that emerged in the nineteenth century is still alive in Oklahoma. Rodeos once functioned as a way for cowboys to keep up their ranching skills. Now, few cowboys use these skills for actual ranching. Instead, they train and compete for cash prizes. Today's rodeos owe some of their traditions to the original Wild West shows, which also included riding and roping demonstrations.

With modern advances, ranching life has changed. Today, many ranchers live with their families in comfortable homes and use less traditional methods in raising cattle. Trucks are more common than horses on the range, and even helicopters may be used to herd cattle.

The Red Earth Festival, which takes place every June in Oklahoma City, is a three-day celebration of Native-American culture.

QUICK FACTS

The drum is a very important part of traditional Native-American dances. A group of people sit around one large drum, strike it, and chant while dances are performed. Many Native Peoples consider the drum to be "the heartbeat of the people."

The Pioneer Days Celebration in Oklahoma is an annual rodeo with over 600 contestants.

Tulsa has a mural that pays tribute to one of its greatest performers at Jazz on Greenwood—Ella Fitzgerald.

African Americans have played an important role in Oklahoma's cultural development, especially in terms of music. Blues, gospel, and jazz can be heard across the state. In the 1920s, jazz boomed in the Second Street area, known as Deep Deuce, in Oklahoma City. Today, people of many different backgrounds come together to celebrate this rich African-American musical heritage by attending jazz, gospel, and blues music festivals, which are held throughout the state.

Jazz lovers can listen to cool tunes every August at Jazz on Greenwood in Tulsa. While in Tulsa, residents and tourists can visit the Oklahoma Jazz Hall of Fame. Blues fans can head to the historic town of Rentiesville to catch the Dusk 'Til Dawn Blues Festival every September.

One of the longest-running African-American rodeos is held each year in Okmulgee.

Many Oklahomans celebrate the Kolache Festival in Prague, Oklahoma and the Czech Festival in Yukon, Oklahoma every year.

The Oklahoma Czech Festival in Yukon takes place on the first Saturday in October. Czech culture is celebrated with traditional foods and dancers.

Native-American beadwork often features animal images.

ARTS AND ENTERTAINMENT

The arts are an important part of Oklahoma's culture. In fact, the law states that the arts must be taught in all schools. Two organizations exist to help keep the arts **accessible** to all state residents: the National Endowment for the Arts and the Oklahoma State Arts Council. Both groups sponsor community arts projects and performances.

Native-American arts and crafts can be found across the state. Traditional crafts such as beadwork, featherwork, and jewelry-making are still practiced. Original crafts and artwork by Native Peoples can be seen at the Southern Plains Indian Museum in Anadarko. Art lovers can also find modern Native-American paintings and sculptures at Muskogee's Five Civilized Tribes Museum.

QUICK FACTS

One of Oklahoma's earliest entertainers was Will Rogers, whose productive movie career began with Wild West shows.

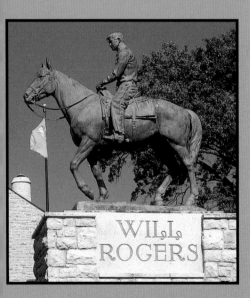

WILL ROGERS

Five famous Native-American ballerinas come from Oklahoma. They are Maria Tallchief, Marjorie Tallchief, Yvonne Chouteau, Moscelyne Larkin, and Rozella Hightower.

The Southern Plains Indian Museum features the work of many Native-American artists. The museum also has a permanent exhibit dedicated to the work of the people of Oklahoma.

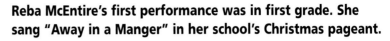

Reba McEntire's first performance was in first grade. She sang "Away in a Manger" in her school's Christmas pageant.

Many world-famous singers and musicians hail from Oklahoma. Some of the state's country and western stars have gone on to become national celebrities in recent years. Country music performers include Garth Brooks from Tulsa, Vince Gill from Norman, and Reba McEntire from McAlester.

Garth Brooks began his music career while attending Oklahoma State University in Stillwater. He started performing at a local club called Tumbleweeds. Vince Gill's music career started earlier than that—he was a member of a high school band. Reba McEntire began singing as a child, in a family band called the Singing McEntires. She sang with her brothers and sisters in clubs and community centers around McAlester. Oklahoma has also produced some first-rate opera singers, including Leona Mitchell, Chris Merritt, and David Pittman-Jennings.

Garth Brooks is one of the most popular country musicians in the nation. He is the first musician to have an album make the Billboard's pop and country charts at the same time.

QUICK FACTS

Some of Oklahoma's highly-acclaimed writers include Ralph Ellison, John Hope Franklin, and Tony Hillerman.

Four huge murals depicting Oklahoma history were painted in the state's capital city by Charles Banks Wilson.

The late folk singer Woody Guthrie was an Oklahoman. He was known for his songs about the Great Depression and the Dust Bowl era.

SPORTS

Oklahoma may not be home to any professional sports teams, but that does not prevent it from producing some incredible athletes. Many of baseball's greats have come from the Sooner State. They include Mickey Mantle, Johnny Bench, Dizzy and Paul Dean, Joe Carter, Darrel Porter, and Warren Spahn.

One of Oklahoma's most famous baseball players and athletes was Jim Thorpe. Thought by many to be the greatest athlete of all time, this Oklahoman of Native-American heritage won eight gold medals at the Olympic Games in 1912. Two of the medals were awarded for the **pentathlon** and **decathlon**. No athlete since has won both competitions in the Olympic Games. However, Thorpe was stripped of his medals because he had played semi-professional baseball before competing in the Olympic Games. Since he had earned money in sports, he was no longer considered an **amateur** athlete. At that time, only amateurs were allowed to compete in the Olympics. But Jim Thorpe did not quit his athletic career. He went on to play both professional baseball and football.

Mickey Mantle is one of the greatest center fielders in the history of baseball, with more home runs than any other switch-hitter.

The legendary Jim Thorpe was voted into the Football Hall of Fame in 1963.

QUICK FACTS

Jim Thorpe was named the greatest athlete of the first half of the twentieth century by the Associated Press.

Former Olympian Nadia Comaneci and her husband, Bart Conner, run a gymnastics school in Conner's home state of Oklahoma.

Oklahomans strongly support their college sports teams. This includes the football and basketball teams at two of the state's largest universities: University of Oklahoma and Oklahoma State University. The Sooners at the University of Oklahoma have seen many football greats, including Steve Owens, Lee Roy Selmon, Brian Bosworth, and Troy Aikman.

Many other top athletes have come from Oklahoma. They include golfer Nancy Lopez Wright, gymnast Shannon Miller, rodeo star Jim Shoulders, and wrestler John Smith. In recent years, Shannon Miller has taken center stage in gymnastics. By the age of twenty, she had won more medals than any other gymnast from the United States. She claimed forty-nine national medals and fifty-eight international medals.

The Oklahoma Sooners have a long tradition of success and have been national champions seven times.

Oklahoma Stadium is the largest sports arena in Oklahoma and is among the largest of all college football stadiums in the United States.

Brain Teasers

1

One African-American cowboy became popular during the days of the Wild West. Who was he?

Answer: Bill Pickett was an expert rider and roper with the Miller Brothers' famous 101 Ranch Wild West Show. Pickett is given credit for inventing bulldogging, which is bringing down a steer by twisting its horns.

2

Where do 10 million crows fly each October?

Answer: They flock to the Fort Cobb Recreation Area in Oklahoma.

3

Where can visitors to Oklahoma learn about the state's early oil boom?

Answer: The Healdton Oil Museum in Healdton, Oklahoma contains artifacts and photographs of Oklahoma's early oil days.

4

The state of Oklahoma is divided into six different regions, aside from the land regions. What are they?

Answer: They are Frontier Country, Green Country, Red Carpet Country, Lake and Trail Country, Kiamichi Country, and Great Plains Country.

5 Name Oklahoma's four mountain ranges.

Answer: They are the Arbuckles, Kiamichis, Ouachitas, and the Wichitas.

6 Which Native-American groups were called the "Five Civilized Tribes"?

Answer: They were the Choctaw, Cherokee, Chickasaw, Creek, and the Seminole.

7 What well-known highway runs through Oklahoma?

Answer: The "main street of America," also known as Route 66, runs for 400 miles through the state.

8 Name writer Ralph Ellison's most popular novel.

Answer: It is called *Invisible Man*. He also wrote *Shadow and Act* and *Going to the Territory*.

FOR MORE INFORMATION

Books

Aylesworth, Thomas and Virginia Aylesworth. *Discovering America: South Central.* New York: Chelsea House, 1996.

Bernotas, Bob. *Jim Thorpe.* New York: Chelsea House, 1993.

Heinrichs, Ann. *Oklahoma.* Chicago: Children's Press, 1989.

Reedy, Jerry. *America the Beautiful: Oklahoma.* Danbury, Connecticut: Children's Press, 1998.

Thompson, Kathleen. *Oklahoma.* Austin: Raintree Steck-Vaughn, 1996.

Web sites

You can also go online and have a look at the following Web sites:

Oklahoma Tourism
http://www.travelok.com

50 States: Oklahoma
http://www.50states.com/oklahoma.htm

About: Oklahoma City
http://oklahomacity.about.com

Oklahoma State
http://www.state.ok.us

Some Web sites stay current longer than others. To find other Oklahoma Web sites, enter search terms, such as "Oklahoma," "Tulsa," "Jim Thorpe," or any other topic you want to research.

GLOSSARY

accessible: easy to approach, available

allotted: set aside for a special purpose

amateur: an athlete who has never competed for financial rewards

archeologists: scientists who study early peoples through artifacts and remains

aviation: the design, development, and production of aircraft

decathlon: an athletic contest that requires competitors to take part in ten different track-and-field events

diverse: varied, having differences

diversified: varied, widely distributed

ethnic: relating to a group of people who share a common race, religion, or culture

fabled: legendary, told in stories

fertile: ground rich in materials for plant growth

heritage: ancestry, a person's cultural background

inducted: admitted as a member

mural: a large painting that is painted directly on a wall or ceiling

Panhandle: a long, narrow strip of land that is connected to a larger territory, such as a state

pentathlon: an athletic contest that requires competitors to take part in five different track-and-field events

powwow: a Native-American ceremony

precipitation: water that falls from the sky as rain, hail, or snow

propose: to offer for consideration

relocated: moved to a new location

revenue: income

tributary: a river or stream that joins a larger river

INDEX